OFFICIAL SQA PAST PAPERS
WITH ANSWERS

HIGHER

ENGLISH
2006-2010

First exam published in 2006.
Published by Bright Red Publishing Ltd, 6 Stafford Street, Edinburgh EH3 7AU
tel: 0131 220 5804 fax: 0131 220 6710 info@brightredpublishing.co.uk www.brightredpublishing.co.uk

ISBN 978-1-84948-136-6

A CIP Catalogue record for this book is available from the British Library.

Bright Red Publishing is grateful to the copyright holders, as credited on the final page of the book, for permission to use their material.
Every effort has been made to trace the copyright holders and to obtain their permission for the use of copyright material.
Bright Red Publishing will be happy to receive information allowing us to rectify any error or omission in future editions.

2006

[BLANK PAGE]

X115/301

| NATIONAL QUALIFICATIONS 2006 | FRIDAY, 12 MAY 9.00 AM – 10.30 AM | ENGLISH HIGHER Close Reading—Text |

There are TWO passages and questions.

Read the passages carefully and then answer all the questions, which are printed in a separate booklet.

You should read the passages to:

understand what the writers are saying about problems of diet and obesity in the modern world (**Understanding—U**);

analyse their choices of language, imagery and structures to recognise how they convey their points of view and contribute to the impact of the passage (**Analysis—A**);

evaluate how effectively they have achieved their purpose (**Evaluation—E**).

SCOTTISH
QUALIFICATIONS
AUTHORITY

PASSAGE 1

The first passage is from an article in The Economist *magazine in December 2003. In it, the writer explores the problem of obesity in the modern world.*

THE SHAPE OF THINGS TO COME

When the world was a simpler place, the rich were fat, the poor were thin, and right-thinking people worried about how to feed the hungry. Now, in much of
5 the world, the rich are thin, the poor are fat, and right-thinking people are worrying about obesity.

Evolution is mostly to blame. It has designed mankind to cope with
10 deprivation, not plenty. People are perfectly tuned to store energy in good years to see them through lean ones. But when bad times never come, they are stuck with that energy, stored around
15 their expanding bellies.

Thanks to rising agricultural productivity, lean years are rarer all over the globe. Pessimistic economists, who used to draw graphs proving that the
20 world was shortly going to run out of food, have gone rather quiet lately. According to the UN, the number of people short of food fell from 920m in 1980 to 799m 20 years later, even though
25 the world's population increased by 1·6 billion over the period. This is mostly a cause for celebration. Mankind has won what was, for most of his time on this planet, his biggest battle: to ensure that
30 he and his offspring had enough to eat. But every silver lining has a cloud, and the consequence of prosperity is a new plague that brings with it a host of interesting policy dilemmas.

35 There is no doubt that obesity is the world's biggest public-health issue today—the main cause of heart disease, which kills more people these days than AIDS, malaria, war; the principal risk
40 factor in diabetes; heavily implicated in cancer and other diseases. Since the World Health Organisation labelled obesity an epidemic in 2000, reports on its fearful consequences have come thick
45 and fast.

Will public-health warnings, combined with media pressure, persuade people to get thinner, just as such warnings finally put them off tobacco? Possibly. In the
50 rich world, sales of healthier foods are booming and new figures suggest that over the past year Americans got very slightly thinner for the first time in recorded history. But even if Americans
55 are losing a few ounces, it will be many years before their country solves the health problems caused by half a century's dining to excess. And everywhere else in the economically
60 developed world, people are still piling on the pounds.

That's why there is now a worldwide consensus among doctors that governments should do something to
65 stop them. There's nothing radical about the idea that governments should intervene in the food business. They've been at it since 1202, when King John of England first banned the adulteration of
70 bread. Governments and the public seem to agree that ensuring the safety and stability of the food supply is part of the state's job. But obesity is a more complicated issue than food safety. It is
75 not about ensuring that people don't get poisoned: it is about changing their behaviour.

Should governments be trying to do anything about it at all?

80 There is one bad reason for doing something, and two good reasons. The bad reason is that governments should help citizens look after themselves. People, the argument goes, are misled by

85 their genes, which are constantly trying to pack away a few more calories just in case of a famine around the corner. Governments should help guide them towards better eating habits. But that

90 argument is weaker in the case of food than it is for tobacco—nicotine is addictive, chocolate is not—and no better than it is in any other area where people have a choice of being sensible or

95 silly. People are constantly torn by the battle between their better and worse selves. It's up to them, not governments, to decide who should win.

A better argument for intervention is

100 that dietary habits are established early in childhood. Once people get fat, it is hard for them to get thin; once they are used to breakfasting on chips and fizzy drinks, that's hard to change. The state, which

105 has some responsibility for moulding minors, should try to ensure that its small citizens aren't mainlining sugar at primary school. Britain's government is gesturing towards tough restrictions on

110 advertising junk food to children. That seems unlikely to have much effect. Sweden already bans advertising to

children, and its young people are as porky as those in comparable countries. Other moves, such as banning junk food 115 from schools, might work better. In some countries, such as America, soft-drinks companies bribe schools to let them install vending machines. That should stop. 120

A second plausible argument for intervention is that thin people subsidise fat people through contributions to the National Health Service. If everybody is forced to carry the weight of the seriously 125 fat, then everybody has an interest in seeing them slim down. That is why some people believe the government should tax fattening food—sweets, snacks and take-aways. They argue this 130 might discourage consumption of unhealthy food and recoup some of the costs of obesity.

It might; but it would also constitute too great an intrusion on liberty for the gain 135 in equity and efficiency it might (or might not) represent. Society has a legitimate interest in fat, because fat and thin people both pay for it. But it also has a legitimate interest in not having the 140 government stick its nose too far into the private sphere. If people want to eat their way to grossness and an early grave, let them.

[Turn over

PASSAGE 2

The second passage appeared as an article in The Observer *newspaper in May 2004. In it, Susie Orbach, a clinician who has worked for many years with people suffering from eating problems, suggests that there are different views on the "obesity epidemic".*

FOOLISH PANIC IS ABOUT PROFIT

At primary school, my son's lunch-box was inspected and found to fail. It contained chocolate biscuits. The school, believing it was doing the right
5 thing, had banned sweets, chocolates and crisps in the name of good nutrition.

After school and in the playground, away from the teachers' eyes, sweets and chocolates were traded. They became
10 the marks of rebellion and the statements of independence. Eating foods they suspected the grown-ups would rather they didn't, made those foods ever so much more enticing. They
15 weren't just food but food plus attitude.

The school was well-meaning—just misguided. Its attitude, like most of what permeates the obesity debate, has turned good intentions into
20 bad conclusions. Despite endless thoughtful discussion on the subject, we are left with a sense that obesity is about to destabilise the NHS, that dangerous fat is swamping the nation.

25 That there is a considerable increase in obesity is not in question. The extent of it is. For many, obesity is a source of anguish and severe health difficulties. But the motivation of some of those who
30 trumpet these dangers associated with obesity needs to be questioned. There is considerable evidence that there is serious money to be made from a condition in search of treatment, and
35 the categorisation of fat may just fit this bill perfectly. In the US, commercial slimming clubs and similar groups contributed millions of dollars to Shape Up America, an organisation which was
40 part of a strategy to turn obesity into a disease which can be treated by the pharmaceutical, diet and medical industries. Medicine is, after all, an industry in the US.

45 So sections of the market aim to profit from the notion that we are all too fat. We need to contest that. It isn't the case. Evidence from the professional journals shows that fitness, not fat,
50 determines our mortality. You can be fat, fit and healthy.

We are in danger of being too willing to mimic the US dogma on the demonisation of fat and of particular
55 foods. This matters because it creates a climate in which the government may fail to ask fundamental questions about whose interests are served by the introduction of hysteria around obesity;
60 particularly who profits and who hurts. A corrective to the scare tactics is needed. People should consider, for example, the simple fact that the new rise in obesity is not simple growth, but
65 is partly due to the body mass index (BMI) being revised downwards in the past six years. If you are Brad Pitt, you are now considered overweight. If you are as substantial as Russell Crowe, you
70 are obese. Overnight 36 million Americans woke up to find that they were obese.

The hidden psychological effects of this attack on our body size are enormous.
75 We are not going to protect the next generation by simply exhorting them to eat so-called good foods.

There is a lot to be done. We need to address what food means in people's emotional lives. We need to transform
80 the culture of thinness. We need to recognise that we as a society are deeply confused about eating and dieting. And we need to realise that part of this confusion has been cynically promoted
85 by those who now are selling us the obesity epidemic.

[END OF TEXT]

X115/302

NATIONAL QUALIFICATIONS 2006	FRIDAY, 12 MAY 9.00 AM – 10.30 AM	**ENGLISH HIGHER** Close Reading–Questions

Answer all questions. **Use your own words whenever possible and particularly when you are instructed to do so.**

50 marks are allocated to this paper.

A code letter (U, A, E) is used alongside each question to give some indication of the skills being assessed. The number of marks attached to each question will give some indication of the length of answer required.

SCOTTISH QUALIFICATIONS AUTHORITY

PB X115/302 6/38870   ©

Questions on Passage 1

Marks   Code

1. Read the first paragraph (lines 1–7).

    (a) Explain briefly how the concerns of "right-thinking people" have changed over time.   **1   U**

    (b) Identify **two** ways by which the sentence structure in these lines emphasises the change.   **2   A**

2. "Evolution is mostly to blame." (line 8)

    How does the writer go on to explain this statement? You should refer to lines 8–15 and use your own words as far as possible.   **2   U**

3. Read lines 16–34.

    (a) Why, according to lines 16–26, have the "pessimistic economists . . . gone rather quiet"?   **1   U**

    (b) "This is mostly a cause for celebration." (lines 26–27)

    What evidence does the writer provide in lines 27–34 to support this statement?   **2   U**

    (c) How effective do you find the imagery of lines 27–34 in illustrating the writer's line of thought? You must refer to **two** examples in your answer.   **4   A/E**

4. How does the writer's language in lines 35–45 stress the seriousness of the health problem?

    In your answer you should refer to at least two features such as sentence structure, word choice, tone . . .   **4   A**

5. Identify from lines 46–61 one cause for hope and one cause for concern. Use your own words as far as possible.   **2   U**

6. In lines 62–133 the writer moves on to discuss the arguments for and against government intervention in the food industry.

    (a) According to lines 62–77, what was the purpose of government intervention in the past, and what is a further purpose of its intervention now?   **2   U**

    (b) Read carefully lines 80–133.

    Summarise the key points of the "one bad reason" and the "two good reasons" (lines 80–81) for government intervention in food policy. You must use your own words as far as possible.   **6   U**

7. In the final paragraph (lines 134–144) the writer makes clear that he disapproves of too much government intervention.

    Show how the writer uses particular features of language to demonstrate his strength of feeling.   **4   A**

    (30)

Questions on Passage 2

Marks Code

8. "The school was well-meaning—just misguided." (lines 16–17)

   (*a*) How do lines 1–15 demonstrate this? 2 U

   (*b*) Show how the writer's word choice in lines 7–15 makes clear the children's attitude to the school's ban. 2 A

9. Read lines 25–44.

   Identify what, according to the writer, is the "motivation" referred to in line 29, and show in your own words how it is illustrated in lines 36–44. 3 U

10. Show how the sentence structure in lines 45–51 highlights the writer's views about the obesity debate. 2 A

11. "A corrective to the scare tactics is needed." (lines 61–62)

    (*a*) Show how the language of lines 52–60 supports the connotation(s) of the expression "scare tactics". 2 A

    (*b*) Explain in your own words how lines 62–72 suggest a "corrective" to the scare tactics. 2 U

12. How does the writer's language in the final paragraph (lines 78–87) highlight her belief that action is required on this issue? 2 A

(15)

Questions on both Passages

13. Consider lines 1–45 of Passage 1 and lines 1–51 of Passage 2.

    In these lines each writer presents the opening stages of an argument about obesity.

    (*a*) Briefly state an important difference between the two **points of view** as set out in these lines. 1 U

    (*b*) By comparing the **style** of these lines, show which you find more effective in capturing your interest. 4 A/E

    (5)

    Total (50)

[END OF QUESTION PAPER]

[BLANK PAGE]

X115/303

NATIONAL
QUALIFICATIONS
2006

FRIDAY, 12 MAY
10.50 AM – 12.20 PM

ENGLISH
HIGHER
Critical Essay

Answer **two** questions.

Each question must be taken from a different section.

Each question is worth 25 marks.

SCOTTISH
QUALIFICATIONS
AUTHORITY

Answer TWO questions from this paper. Each question must be chosen from a different Section (A–E). You are not allowed to choose two questions from the same Section.

In all Sections you may use Scottish texts.

Write the number of each question in the margin of your answer booklet.

You should spend about 45 minutes on each essay.

The following will be assessed:

- the relevance of your essays to the questions you have chosen, and the extent to which you sustain an appropriate line of thought

- your knowledge and understanding of key elements, central concerns and significant details of the chosen texts, supported by detailed and relevant evidence

- your understanding, as appropriate to the questions chosen, of how relevant aspects of structure/style/language contribute to the meaning/effect/impact of the chosen texts, supported by detailed and relevant evidence

- your evaluation, as appropriate to the questions chosen, of the effectiveness of the chosen texts, supported by detailed and relevant evidence

- the quality of your written expression and the technical accuracy of your writing.

SECTION A—DRAMA

Answers to questions on drama should address relevantly the central concern(s)/theme(s) of the text and be supported by reference to appropriate dramatic techniques such as: conflict, characterisation, key scene(s), dialogue, climax, exposition, dénouement, structure, plot, setting, aspects of staging (such as lighting, music, stage set, stage directions . . .), soliloquy, monologue . . .

1. Choose a play in which the dramatist's use of contrast between two characters is important to your understanding of one of them.

   Discuss how your understanding of this character is strengthened by the contrast.

2. Choose a play in which the conclusion leaves you with mixed emotions but clearly conveys the dramatist's message.

   Briefly explain how the mixed emotions are aroused by the conclusion and then discuss how you are given a clear understanding of the message of the play as a whole.

3. Choose a play which underlines how one person's flaw(s) can have a significant impact on other people as well as on himself or herself.

   Explain briefly the nature of the flaw(s) and then, in detail, assess how much the character and others are affected.

4. Choose a play in which an important theme is effectively highlighted by one specific scene or incident.

   Explain how the theme is explored in the play as a whole and then show in detail how the chosen scene or incident effectively highlights it.

SECTION B—PROSE

Prose Fiction

Answers to questions on prose fiction should address relevantly the central concern(s)/theme(s) of the text(s) and be supported by reference to appropriate techniques of prose fiction such as: characterisation, setting, key incident(s), narrative technique, symbolism, structure, climax, plot, atmosphere, dialogue, imagery . . .

5. Choose a **novel** or **short story** in which a central character's failure to understand the reality of his or her situation is an important feature of the text.

   Explain how the writer makes you aware of this failure and show how it is important to your appreciation of the text as a whole.

6. Choose a **novel**, set in a time different from your own, with a theme relevant to the world today.

   Show how you are led to an appreciation of the theme's continuing relevance, despite its setting in time.

7. Choose a **novel** or **short story** which you feel has a particularly well-chosen title.

   Explain why you think the title helps you to appreciate the central idea(s) of the text.

8. Choose a **novel** in which a key incident involves rejection or disappointment or loss.

   Describe briefly the key incident and assess its significance to the text as a whole.

Prose Non-fiction

Answers to questions on prose non-fiction should address relevantly the central concern(s)/theme(s) of the text and be supported by reference to appropriate techniques of prose non-fiction such as: ideas, use of evidence, selection of detail, point of view, stance, setting, anecdote, narrative voice, style, language, structure, organisation of material . . .

9. Choose an **essay** or **piece of journalism** which has made an impact on you because of its effective style.

   Discuss how the writer's style adds to the impact of the content.

10. Choose a **non-fiction text** which provides insight into a country or a personality or a lifestyle.

    Describe briefly the country or personality or lifestyle and discuss the means by which the writer leads you to this insight.

11. Choose a **non-fiction text** which explores a significant aspect of political or cultural life.

    Show how the writer's presentation enhances your understanding of the chosen aspect of political or cultural life.

[Turn over

SECTION C—POETRY

Answers to questions on poetry should address relevantly the central concern(s)/theme(s) of the text(s) and be supported by reference to appropriate poetic techniques such as: imagery, verse form, structure, mood, tone, sound, rhythm, rhyme, characterisation, contrast, setting, symbolism, word choice . . .

12. Choose a poem in which there is a noticeable change of mood at one or more than one point in the poem.

    Show how the poet conveys the change(s) of mood and discuss the importance of the change(s) to the central idea of the poem.

13. Choose a poem which deals with a childhood experience.

    Discuss to what extent the poet's description of the experience leads you to a clear understanding of the poem's theme.

14. Choose **two** poems by the same poet which you consider similar in theme and style.

    By referring to theme and style in both poems, discuss which poem you prefer.

15. Choose a poem which explores one of the following subjects: bravery, compassion, tenderness.

    Show how the poet's exploration of the subject appeals to you emotionally and/or intellectually.

SECTION D—FILM AND TV DRAMA

> *Answers to questions on film and TV drama should address relevantly the central concern(s)/theme(s) of the text(s) and be supported by reference to appropriate techniques of film and TV drama such as: key sequence(s), characterisation, conflict, structure, plot, dialogue, editing/montage, sound/soundtrack, aspects of mise-en-scène (such as lighting, colour, use of camera, costume, props . . .), mood, setting, casting, exploitation of genre . . .*

16. Choose a **film** or ***TV drama** the success of which is built on a central figure carefully constructed to appeal to a particular audience.

    Show how the film or programme makers construct this figure and explain why he/she/it appeals to that particular audience.

17. Choose a **film** or ***TV drama** in which a power struggle shapes the lives of key characters and/or groups.

    Discuss how effectively the film or programme makers establish the power struggle and go on to explain how it shapes the lives of the key characters and/or groups.

18. Choose a **film** in which the film makers have presented an epic story to critical and/or box office acclaim.

    Show how the film makers convey key epic elements and explain why you think the film has received such acclaim.

19. Choose a **film** or ***TV drama** which is based on a novel and successfully captures such elements of the book as setting, character, mood and theme.

    Show how the film or programme makers successfully capture any two elements of the novel.

*"TV drama" includes a single play, a series or a serial.

[Turn over

SECTION E—LANGUAGE

> *Answers to questions on language should address relevantly the central concern(s) of the language research/study and be supported by reference to appropriate language concepts such as: register, jargon, tone, vocabulary, word choice, technical terminology, presentation, illustration, accent, grammar, idiom, slang, dialect, structure, vocabulary, point of view, orthography, abbreviation . . .*

20. Consider the use of language to influence public opinion.

Identify some of the ways in which language is used to influence the public's view on an issue of public interest. Evaluate the success of at least two of these ways.

21. Consider some of the differences between spoken language used in informal contexts and spoken language used in formal contexts.

Identify some of the areas of difference and show to what extent the different forms are effective for the contexts in which they are used.

22. Consider the language—spoken or written—which is typically used by a group of people with a common leisure or vocational interest.

To what extent is the specialist language effective in:

- describing the details and procedures connected with the group's common interest and/or

- reinforcing the interaction within the group?

23. Consider any one electronic means of communication introduced over the last forty years or so.

To what extent has your chosen means of communication developed its own form of language? By examining aspects of this language discuss what you feel are its advantages and/or disadvantages.

[END OF QUESTION PAPER]

[BLANK PAGE]

X115/301

NATIONAL QUALIFICATIONS 2007	FRIDAY, 11 MAY 9.00 AM – 10.30 AM	**ENGLISH** HIGHER Close Reading—Text

There are TWO passages and questions.

Read the passages carefully and then answer all the questions, which are printed in a separate booklet.

You should read the passages to:

understand what the writers are saying about the proposal to put online the contents of some major libraries (**Understanding—U**);

analyse their choices of language, imagery and structures to recognise how they convey their points of view and contribute to the impact of the passage (**Analysis—A**);

evaluate how effectively they have achieved their purpose (**Evaluation—E**).

SCOTTISH
QUALIFICATIONS
AUTHORITY

PASSAGE 1

In the first passage George Kerevan, writing in The Scotsman *newspaper in December 2003, responds to the prospect of an "online library".*

DESPITE GOOGLE, WE STILL NEED GOOD LIBRARIES

The internet search engine Google, with whom I spend more time than with my loved ones, is planning to put the contents of the world's greatest university libraries online, including the Bodleian in Oxford and those of Harvard and Stanford in America. Part of me is ecstatic at the thought of all that information at my
5 fingertips; another part of me is nostalgic, because I think physical libraries, book-lined and cathedral-quiet, are a cherished part of civilisation we lose at our cultural peril.

My love affair with libraries started early, in the Drumchapel housing scheme in the Fifties. For the 60,000 exiles packed off from slum housing to the city's outer
10 fringe, Glasgow Council neglected the shops and amenities but somehow remembered to put in a public library—actually, a wooden shed. That library was split into two—an adult section and a children's section. This was an early taste of forbidden fruit. Much useful human reproductive knowledge was gained from certain books examined surreptitiously in the adult biology section.

15 At university, I discovered the wonder of the library as a physical space. Glasgow University has a skyscraper library, built around a vast atrium stretching up through the various floors. Each floor was devoted to a different subject classification. Working away on the economics floor, I could see other students above or below—chatting, flirting, doodling, panicking—all cocooned in their own separate
20 worlds of knowledge. Intrigued, I soon took to exploring what was on these other planets: science, architecture, even a whole floor of novels. The unique aspect of a physical library is that you can discover knowledge by accident. There are things you know you don't know, but there are also things you never imagined you did not know.

25 There is a stock response to my love affair with libraries: that I am being too nostalgic. That the multi-tasking, MTV generation can access information from a computer, get cheap books from the supermarket and still chatter to each other at a thousand decibels. Who needs old-fashioned library buildings? And why should councils subsidise what Google will provide for free?

30 There is some proof for this line of argument. The number of people in Scotland using their local public library falls every year, with just under a quarter of Scots now borrowing books (admittedly, that was 34 million books). As a result, local authorities have reduced their funding for new books by 30 per cent. Of course, fewer new books mean fewer library users, so guaranteeing the downward spiral.

35 It may well be that public demand and technical change mean we no longer need the dense neighbourhood network of local libraries of yore. But our culture, local and universal, does demand strategically situated libraries where one can find the material that is too expensive for the ordinary person to buy, or too complex to find online. Such facilities are worth funding publicly because the return in informed
40 citizenship and civic pride is far in excess of the money spent.

Libraries also have that undervalued resource—the trained librarian. The ultimate Achilles' heel of the internet is that it presents every page of information as being

equally valid, which is of course nonsense. The internet is cluttered with false information, or just plain junk. The library, with its collection honed and developed
45 by experts, is a guarantee of the quality and veracity of the information contained therein, something that Google can never provide.

Libraries have another function still, which the internet cannot fulfil. Libraries, like museums, are custodians of knowledge—and should be funded as such. It has become the fashion in recent decades to turn our great national libraries and
50 museums into entertainment centres, with audio-visuals, interactive displays and gimmicks. While I have some enthusiasm for popularising esoteric knowledge, it cannot always be reduced to the level of a child's view of the universe. We have a duty to future generations to invest in the custodians of our culture, in particular its literature and manuscripts.

55 Of course, I can't wait for Google to get online with the Bodleian Library's one million books. Yet here's one other thing I learned from a physical library space: the daunting scale of human knowledge and our inability to truly comprehend even a fraction of it. On arriving at Glasgow University library, I did a quick calculation of how many economics books there were on the shelves and realised that I could
60 not read them all. Ever. From which realisation comes the beginning of wisdom—and that is very different from merely imbibing information.

PASSAGE 2

In the second passage Ben Macintyre, writing in The Times newspaper, also in December 2003, responds to the same news, and considers the future of the "traditional library".

PARADISE IS PAPER, PARCHMENT AND DUST

I have a halcyon library memory. I am sitting under a cherry tree in the tiny central courtyard of the Cambridge University Library, a book in one hand and an almond slice in the other. On the grass beside me is an incredibly pretty girl. We are surrounded by eight million books. Behind the walls on every side of the
5 courtyard, the books stretch away in compact ranks hundreds of yards deep, the shelves extending at the rate of two miles a year. There are books beneath us in the subterranean stacks, and they reach into the sky; we are entombed in words, an unimaginable volume of collected knowledge in cold storage, quiet and vast and waiting.

10 Perhaps that was the moment I fell in love with libraries.

Or perhaps it was earlier, growing up in Scotland, when the mobile library would lurch up the road with stocks of Enid Blyton for the kids and supplies of bodice-rippers on the top shelf with saucy covers, to be giggled over when the driver-librarian was having his cup of tea.

15 Or perhaps the moment came earlier yet, when my father took me deep into the Bodleian in Oxford and I inhaled, for the first time, that intoxicating mixture of paper, parchment and dust.

I have spent a substantial portion of my life since in libraries, and I still enter them with a mixture of excitement and awe. I am not alone in this. Veneration for
20 libraries is as old as writing itself, for a library is more to our culture than a

collection of books: it is a temple, a symbol of power, the hushed core of civilisation, the citadel of memory, with its own mystique, social and sensual as well as intellectual.

But now a revolution, widely compared to the invention of printing itself, is taking 25 place among the book shelves, and the library will never be the same again. This week Google announced plans to digitise fifteen million books from five great libraries, including the Bodleian.

Some fear that this total library, vast and invisible, could finally destroy traditional libraries, which will become mere warehouses for the physical objects, empty of 30 people and life. However, the advantages of a single scholarly online catalogue are incalculable and rather than destroying libraries, the internet will protect the written word as never before, and render knowledge genuinely democratic. Fanatics always attack the libraries first, dictators seek to control the literature, elites hoard the knowledge that is power. Shi Huangdi, the Chinese emperor of the 3rd century BC, 35 ordered that all literature, history and philosophy written before the founding of his dynasty should be destroyed. More books were burnt in the 20th century than any other—in Nazi Germany, Bosnia and Afghanistan. With the online library, the books will finally be safe, and the bibliophobes will have been beaten, for ever.

But will we bother to browse the shelves when we can merely summon up any book 40 in the world with the push of a button? Are the days of the library as a social organism over? Almost certainly not, for reasons psychological and, ultimately, spiritual. Locating a book online is one thing, reading it is quite another, for there is no aesthetic substitute for the physical object; the computer revolution rolls on inexorably, but the world is reading more paper books than ever.

45 And the traditional library will also survive, because a library is central to our understanding of what it is to be human. Libraries are not just for reading in, but for sociable thinking, exploring and exchanging ideas. They were never silent. Technology will not change that, for even in the starchiest heyday of Victorian self-improvement, libraries were intended to be meeting places of the mind, recreational 50 as well as educational. The Openshaw branch of the Manchester public library was built complete with a billiard room. Of course just as bookshops have become trendy, offering brain food and cappuccinos, so libraries, under financial and cultural pressure, will have to evolve by more actively welcoming people in to wander and explore . . . and fall in love.

55 Bookish types have always feared change and technology, but the book, and the library, have adapted and endured, retaining their essential magic. Even Hollywood understood. In the 1957 film *Desk Set*, Katherine Hepburn plays a librarian-researcher whose job is threatened by a computer expert (Spencer Tracy) introducing new technology. In the end, the computer turns out to be an asset, not a 60 danger, Tracy and Hepburn end up smooching, and everyone reads happily ever after.

The marriage of Google and the Bodleian will surely be the same.

[END OF TEXT]

X115/302

NATIONAL
QUALIFICATIONS
2007

FRIDAY, 11 MAY
9.00 AM – 10.30 AM

ENGLISH
HIGHER
Close Reading–Questions

Answer all questions. **Use your own words whenever possible and particularly when you are instructed to do so.**

50 marks are allocated to this paper.

A code letter (U, A, E) is used alongside each question to give some indication of the skills being assessed. The number of marks attached to each question will give some indication of the length of answer required.

SCOTTISH
QUALIFICATIONS
AUTHORITY

Questions on Passage 1

Marks Code

1. Read lines 1–7.

   (a) What two contrasting emotions does the writer have about the plan to put the great university libraries online? Use your own words in your answer.

   2 U

   (b) How does the writer's word choice in these lines help to convey his view of the importance of "physical libraries" (line 5)? Refer to **two** examples in your answer.

   2 A

2. In your opinion, does the writer think Glasgow Council gave the library in Drumchapel a high priority? Justify your answer by close reference to lines 8–14.

   2 U/E

3. Show how the writer uses imagery **and** word choice in lines 15–24 to convey the "wonder of the library as a physical space".

   4 A

4. Read lines 25–34.

   (a) Show how the writer's language in lines 25–29 conveys his attitude to the "MTV generation". You should refer in your answer to such features as sentence structure, word choice, tone . . .

   3 A

   (b) Explain the "downward spiral" (line 34) to which the writer refers.

   1 U

5. (a) In your own words as far as possible, give **four** reasons the writer presents in lines 35–46 in favour of maintaining traditional public libraries.

   4 U

   (b) Show how the writer's word choice in lines 41–46 emphasises the contrast between his attitude to libraries and his attitude to the internet.

   2 A

6. Read lines 47–54.

   (a) Twice in this paragraph the writer refers to libraries as "custodians". What does this word mean?

   1 U

   (b) Show how the language of lines 47–54 suggests that the writer has some reservations about the entertainment aspect of present day libraries and museums.

   2 A

7. How effective do you find the ideas and/or language of the final paragraph (lines 55–61) as a conclusion to the passage as a whole?

   3 E

   (26)

Questions on Passage 2 *Marks Code*

8. Read lines 1–17.

   (*a*) Briefly describe the mood created in lines 1–3 ("I have . . . girl."). 1 U

   (*b*) Show how the writer's use of language in lines 3–9 ("We are . . . waiting.") conveys a sense of awe. 3 A

   (*c*) How effective do you find the repetition of "perhaps" (lines 10–17) in conveying the writer's recollections about libraries? 2 A/E

9. By referring to **one** example, show how the writer's imagery in lines 18–23 conveys the importance of libraries. 2 A

10. Read lines 24–38.

    In your own words as far as possible, explain:

    (*a*) what, according to the writer, the potential disadvantage of the online library is; 1 U

    (*b*) what, according to the writer, the advantages of the online library are. 3 U

11. Read lines 39–54.

    (*a*) Explain what the writer means by "there is no aesthetic substitute for the physical object" (lines 42–43). 2 U

    (*b*) Using your own words as far as possible, explain why the writer believes libraries will "survive" (line 45). 2 U

12. How effectively does the writer use the reference to the film *Desk Set* to conclude the passage in a pleasing way? Refer in your answer to the ideas and language of lines 55–62. 3 E

    (19)

Question on both Passages

13. Which of the two writers do you think presents the more persuasive argument in favour of public libraries?

    Justify your choice by referring to the **ideas and style** of **both** passages. 5 E

    (5)

    Total (50)

[END OF QUESTION PAPER]

[BLANK PAGE]

X115/303

NATIONAL
QUALIFICATIONS
2007

FRIDAY, 11 MAY
10.50 AM – 12.20 PM

ENGLISH

HIGHER
Critical Essay

Answer **two** questions.

Each question must be taken from a different section.

Each question is worth 25 marks.

SCOTTISH
QUALIFICATIONS
AUTHORITY

©

Answer TWO questions from this paper. Each question must be chosen from a different Section (A–E). You are not allowed to choose two questions from the same Section.

In all Sections you may use Scottish texts.

Write the number of each question in the margin of your answer booklet and begin each essay on a fresh page.

You should spend about 45 minutes on each essay.

The following will be assessed:

- the relevance of your essays to the questions you have chosen, and the extent to which you sustain an appropriate line of thought

- your knowledge and understanding of key elements, central concerns and significant details of the chosen texts, supported by detailed and relevant evidence

- your understanding, as appropriate to the questions chosen, of how relevant aspects of structure/style/language contribute to the meaning/effect/impact of the chosen texts, supported by detailed and relevant evidence

- your evaluation, as appropriate to the questions chosen, of the effectiveness of the chosen texts, supported by detailed and relevant evidence

- the quality of your written expression and the technical accuracy of your writing.

SECTION A—DRAMA

Answers to questions on drama should address relevantly the central concern(s)/theme(s) of the text and be supported by reference to appropriate dramatic techniques such as: conflict, characterisation, key scene(s), dialogue, climax, exposition, dénouement, structure, plot, setting, aspects of staging (such as lighting, music, stage set, stage directions . . .), soliloquy, monologue . . .

1. Choose a play which has a theme of revenge or betrayal or sacrifice.

   Show how the dramatist explores your chosen theme and discuss how this treatment enhances your appreciation of the play as a whole.

2. Choose from a play an important scene which you found particularly entertaining or particularly shocking.

   Explain briefly why the scene is important to the play as a whole and discuss in detail how the dramatist makes the scene so entertaining or shocking.

3. Choose a play in which a character makes a crucial error.

   Explain what the error is and discuss to what extent it is important to your understanding of the character's situation in the play as a whole.

4. Choose a play in which the relationship between a male and a female character changes significantly.

   Show how the relationship between the two characters changes and discuss to what extent this illuminates a central idea of the play.

SECTION B—PROSE

Prose Fiction

Answers to questions on prose fiction should address relevantly the central concern(s)/theme(s) of the text(s) and be supported by reference to appropriate techniques of prose fiction such as: characterisation, setting, key incident(s), narrative technique, symbolism, structure, climax, plot, atmosphere, dialogue, imagery . . .

5. Choose a **novel** in which a character reaches a crisis point.

   Explain briefly how this point is reached and go on to discuss how the character's response to the situation extends your understanding of him/her.

6. Choose **two short stories** in which aspects of style contribute significantly to the exploration of theme.

   Compare the ways in which stylistic features are used to create and maintain your interest in the central ideas of the texts.

7. Choose a **novel** with an ending which you found unexpected.

   Explain briefly in what way the ending is unexpected and go on to discuss to what extent it is a satisfactory conclusion to the novel.

8. Choose a **novel** or **short story** in which one of the main characters is not in harmony with her/his society.

   Describe the character's situation and go on to discuss how it adds to your understanding of a central concern of the text.

Prose Non-fiction

Answers to questions on prose non-fiction should address relevantly the central concern(s)/theme(s) of the text and be supported by reference to appropriate techniques of prose non-fiction such as: ideas, use of evidence, selection of detail, point of view, stance, setting, anecdote, narrative voice, style, language, structure, organisation of material . . .

9. Choose a work of **non-fiction** which deals with **travel** or **exploration** or **discovery**.

   Discuss to what extent the presentation of the text reveals as much about the writer's personality and/or views as it does about the subject matter.

10. Choose a **biography** or **autobiography** in which the life of the subject is presented in an effective and engaging way.

    Show how the writer uses techniques of non-fiction to achieve this.

11. Choose an **essay** or **piece of journalism** which appeals to you because it is both informative and passionate.

    Explain what you learned about the topic and discuss how the writer's presentation conveys his/her passion.

[Turn over

SECTION C—POETRY

Answers to questions on poetry should address relevantly the central concern(s)/theme(s) of the text(s) and be supported by reference to appropriate poetic techniques such as: imagery, verse form, structure, mood, tone, sound, rhythm, rhyme, characterisation, contrast, setting, symbolism, word choice . . .

12. Choose a poem in which there is a sinister atmosphere or person or place.

Show how the poet evokes this sinister quality and discuss how it adds to your appreciation of the poem.

13. Choose **two** poems on the same theme which impress you for different reasons.

Compare the treatment of the theme in the two poems and discuss to what extent you find one more impressive than the other.

14. Choose a poem in which there is effective use of one or more of the following: verse form, rhythm, rhyme, repetition, sound.

Show how the poet effectively uses the feature(s) to enhance your appreciation of the poem as a whole.

15. Choose a poem involving a journey which is both literal and metaphorical.

Discuss how effectively the poet describes the journey and makes you aware of its deeper significance.

SECTION D—FILM AND TV DRAMA

> *Answers to questions on film and TV drama should address relevantly the central concern(s)/theme(s) of the text(s) and be supported by reference to appropriate techniques of film and TV drama such as: key sequence(s), characterisation, conflict, structure, plot, dialogue, editing/montage, sound/soundtrack, aspects of mise-en-scène (such as lighting, colour, use of camera, costume, props . . .), mood, setting, casting, exploitation of genre . . .*

16. Choose a **film** or **TV drama*** the success of which is built on a rivalry or friendship between two characters.

    Show how the film or programme makers construct the characters and discuss how the rivalry or friendship contributes to the success of the text.

17. Choose a **film** in which music makes a significant contribution to the impact of the film as a whole.

    Show how the film makers make use of music, and go on to explain how its contribution is so important relative to other elements of the text.

18. Choose a **film** or **TV version** of a stage play or of a novel.

    By referring to key elements of the film or TV version, explain to what extent you think the film or programme makers were successful in transferring the play or novel to the screen.

19. Choose a **film** or **TV drama*** in which setting and atmosphere contribute more than plot to your appreciation of the text.

    Justify your opinion by referring to these elements of the text.

*"TV drama" includes a single play, a series or a serial.

[Turn over

SECTION E—LANGUAGE

> *Answers to questions on language should address relevantly the central concern(s) of the language research/study and be supported by reference to appropriate language concepts such as: register, jargon, tone, vocabulary, word choice, technical terminology, presentation, illustration, accent, grammar, idiom, slang, dialect, structure, point of view, orthography, abbreviation . . .*

20. Consider the spoken or written language of a particular geographical area. (This could be, for example, a village, a city, or a larger area of the UK.)

Identify what is distinctive about the language and evaluate the effects of these distinctive usages on the communication of the people of that area.

21. Consider the language of popular entertainment in the 21st century—in TV, radio, music, magazines, for example.

Describe how the idioms and vocabulary popularised by the entertainment industry influence the everyday speech of the younger generation. Discuss to what extent these usages enrich everyday communication.

22. Consider the language of persuasion employed in a commercial, political, social or personal situation.

Identify and discuss the effectiveness of several ways in which the language you have chosen attempts to be persuasive.

23. Consider the language typical of any particular vocational or interest group with which you are familiar.

To what extent are the specialist terms and idioms typical of this group a barrier to the ability of the general public to understand the communication? How necessary do you think these terms and idioms are for effective communication within the group?

[END OF QUESTION PAPER]

2008

[BLANK PAGE]

X115/301

| NATIONAL QUALIFICATIONS 2008 | THURSDAY, 15 MAY 9.00 AM – 10.30 AM | ENGLISH HIGHER Close Reading—Text |

There are TWO passages and questions.

Read the passages carefully and then answer all the questions, which are printed in a separate booklet.

You should read the passages to:

understand what the writers are saying about the countryside and those who campaign to protect it (**Understanding—U**);

analyse their choices of language, imagery and structures to recognise how they convey their points of view and contribute to the impact of the passage (**Analysis—A**);

evaluate how effectively they have achieved their purpose (**Evaluation—E**).

PASSAGE 1

In this extract from his book "Shades of Green", David Sinclair looks at attitudes to the countryside and discusses to what extent it is part of "our heritage".

RURAL MANIA

The "countryside debate" has rarely been out of the news in Britain in recent years. Reading the newspapers, watching television, listening to the radio, entering a bookshop, one could be forgiven for thinking that we still live in small peasant communities dependent upon the minutest shift in agricultural policy. Sometimes it
5 has seemed almost as if we were still in the early nineteenth century when we relied on the countryside to survive, so extensive have been the debates, so fierce the passions aroused.

One faction has cried constantly that the countryside is in mortal danger from greedy developers whose only motive is profit; another has kept on roaring that
10 farmers are killing every wild thing in sight and threatening the very soil on which we stand through overuse of machinery and chemicals; still another has been continually heard ululating over a decline in the bird population, or the loss of hedgerows, or the disappearance of marshland, or the appearance of coniferous forest.

15 Then there is the proliferation of action groups dedicated to stopping construction of roads, airports, railway lines, factories, shopping centres and houses in rural areas, while multifarious organisations have become accustomed to expending their time and energies in monitoring and reporting on the state of grassland, water, trees, moorlands, uplands, lowlands, birds' eggs, wildflowers, badgers, historical sites and
20 countless other aspects of the landscape and its inhabitants.

It might be thought—indeed, it is widely assumed—that it must be good for the countryside to be returned to the central position it enjoyed in British life long ago. Yet there is a particularly worrying aspect of the new rural mania that suggests it might finally do the countryside more harm than good.

25 This is the identification, in the current clamour, of the countryside in general and the landscape in particular with the past—the insistence on the part of those who claim to have the best intentions of ruralism at heart that their aim is to protect what they glibly refer to as "our heritage". This wildly over-used term is seriously misleading, not least because nobody appears ever to have asked what it means.

30 The assumption is that the landscape is our living link with our history, the visible expression of our British roots, and that if we allow it to change ("to be destroyed", the conservationists would say), the link is broken forever. This view is palpably nonsensical. Our national identity is not defined by the landscape against which we carry on our lives. There is, in fact, no single thread that can be identified as our
35 rural heritage or tradition. Rather there is a bewildering array of different influences that have combined haphazardly through the centuries as successive invaders and immigrants and, later, successive generations, have reconstructed the landscape according to their own needs and ideas. What the conservationists seek to preserve is simply the landscape *as it is now*, in its incarnation of the early twenty-
40 first century. Far from affirming history, this approach actually denies it, for it would remove the continuous change without which history does not exist.

Where, for example, does the "traditional" landscape begin and end? If we take the period when the British Isles were born, nearly 8,000 years ago, we discover that the

conifers so hated by the conservationists today were one of the most important
45 features of the scenery; the "English" oak and the much-loved elm were later
immigrants from the warmer south. As for fauna, our "traditional" species included
reindeer, rhinoceros, bison, hippopotamus and elephant. But where are they now?

Perhaps we should do better in the search for our heritage to consider what the
countryside looked like when man first appeared in what we think of as Britain.
50 That would take us back 35,000 years, to the emergence of our ancestor *Homo
sapiens*, who found himself in an Arctic landscape of ice and tundra. The remnants
of that traditional scene can be found only in the highest mountains of Scotland; the
rest of Britain has changed beyond recognition.

Obviously, then, we must look at more recent times if we are to discover identifiable
55 traditional elements in the landscape we now see about us. Yet if we do that, further
difficulties emerge. The retreat of the last glaciation almost 11,000 years ago was
accompanied by a relatively rapid warming of the climate, which gradually
converted the open Arctic tundra into dense forest. This presented a serious
challenge to Stone Age man, who began to find that the grazing animals, which he
60 hunted for food, were disappearing as their habitat retreated before the encroaching
trees. In order to survive, he was forced to turn increasingly from hunting to
farming, with the dramatic effects on flora and fauna that remain familiar to us
today. As the quality of prehistoric tools improved, some stretches of forest were
felled to provide grazing for domesticated animals, while grasses and cereals were
65 deliberately encouraged because of their usefulness to man. Even the shape of the
countryside was changed as mining began to cut into hillsides, and in some places
soil deterioration set in as the growing populations demanded perhaps the earliest
form of intensive farming. In other words, the chief influence on the landscape of
these islands was not nature but mankind.

PASSAGE 2

*In the second passage, the journalist Richard Morrison responds to criticism of a Government
plan to allow a million new houses to be built in southeast England.*

PULLING UP THE DRAWBRIDGE

The English middle classes are rarely more hypocritical than when waxing
indignant about "the threat to the countryside". What anguishes them usually
turns out to be the threat to their own pleasure or to the value of their property.
And I write those sentences with the heavy heart of a class traitor, for I am a
5 middle-class, middle-aged property owner who has smugly watched his own house
soar in value as more and more young househunters desperately chase fewer and
fewer properties. I am inordinately proud of my view across the green belt (from
an upstairs window admittedly, because of the motorway flyover in between). And
I intend to spend the weekend rambling across the rural England I have loved since
10 boyhood.

The most cherished credo of the English middle classes is that the verdant hills
and dales of the Home Counties should remain forever sacrosanct, and that the
Government's "Stalinist" decision to impose a million extra houses on southeast
England is the most hideous threat to our way of life since the Luftwaffe made its
15 energetic contribution to British town and country planning in 1940. Thousands

of green acres will be choked by concrete, as rapacious housebuilders devour whole landscapes. England's cherished green belts—the 14 great rings of protected fields that have stopped our major cities from sprawling outward for more than half a century—will be swept away.

20 Yet if you sweep away the apoplectic froth and the self-interested posturing and look at the reality, the "threat to the countryside" recedes dramatically. Yes, we do occupy a crowded little island. But what makes it seem crowded is that 98 per cent of us live on 7 per cent of the land. Britain is still overwhelmingly green. Just 11 per cent of our nation is classified as urban.

25 Moreover, planners reckon that as much as a quarter of the green belt around London is wasteland, largely devoid of landscape beauty. So why not use it to relieve the intolerable pressure on affordable housing in the capital? Because that would contravene the long-held myth that green belts are vital "lungs" for cities. Well, lungs they might be. But they benefit chiefly those who live in nice houses 30 inside the green belts (not least by keeping their property values sky-high); and then those who live in nice houses in the leafy outer suburbs; and not at all the people who need the fresh air most: those on inner-city estates.

The green-belt protectionists claim to be saving unspoilt countryside from the rampant advance of bulldozers. Exactly what unspoilt countryside do they imagine 35 they are saving? Primordial forest, unchanged since Boadicea thrashed the Romans? Hogwash. The English have been making and remaking their landscape for millennia to suit the needs of each passing generation.

These protectionists are fond of deriding any housebuilding targets set by the Government as monstrous, Soviet-style diktats. Good grief, what on earth do they 40 imagine that the planning laws protecting green belts and agricultural land are, if not Government interventions that have had a huge, and often disastrous, impact not just on the property market, but on employment, on transport, on public services and on economic growth?

And, of course, on homelessness. Every time a bunch of middle-class homeowners 45 fights off the "intrusion" of a new housing estate into their cherished landscape, they make it more difficult for the young and the poor to find somewhere to live in reasonable proximity to where they can find work. This is the 21st-century equivalent of pulling up the drawbridge after one's own family and friends are safely inside the castle.

[END OF TEXT]

X115/302

NATIONAL
QUALIFICATIONS
2008

THURSDAY, 15 MAY
9.00 AM – 10.30 AM

ENGLISH

HIGHER
Close Reading–Questions

Answer all questions. **Use your own words whenever possible and particularly when you are instructed to do so.**

50 marks are allocated to this paper.

A code letter (U, A, E) is used alongside each question to give some indication of the skills being assessed. The number of marks attached to each question will give some indication of the length of answer required.

Questions on Passage 1

Marks Code

1. Read lines 1–7.

   Explain in your own words why the writer seems surprised that there is so much coverage of the "countryside debate". (line 1)   2   U

2. (*a*) Show how the word choice **and** sentence structure in lines 8–14 emphasise the strong feelings of those who feel the countryside is under threat.   4   A

   (*b*) Show how the writer's use of language in lines 15–20 conveys his disapproval of the "action groups".   2   A

3. Read lines 21–29.

   (*a*) By referring to specific words or phrases, show how lines 21–24 perform a linking function at this stage in the writer's argument.   2   U

   (*b*) Referring to lines 25–29, explain in your own words what the writer believes to be a "particularly worrying aspect of the new rural mania" (line 23).   2   U

4. "This view is palpably nonsensical." (lines 32–33)

   (*a*) Explain, using your own words as far as possible, what "this view" is. Refer to lines 30–32 in your answer.   2   U

   (*b*) Give in your own words **one** of the writer's reasons in lines 33–38 (". . . ideas.") for believing that the view is "palpably nonsensical".   2   U

   (*c*) Show how the writer's use of language in lines 38–41 reinforces his criticism of the conservationists' ideas.   2   A

5. Read lines 42–53.

   Give, in your own words as far as possible, any **three** reasons why it is difficult to define the "traditional" British landscape.   3   U

6. "This presented a serious challenge to Stone Age man . . ." (lines 58–59)

   (*a*) Explain in your own words what the "challenge" was. Refer to lines 54–61 (". . . trees.") in your answer.   2   U

   (*b*) Explain in your own words how Stone Age man responded to the challenge. Refer to lines 61–69 in your answer.   2   U

   (25)

Questions on Passage 2

Marks   Code

7. (*a*) By referring to lines 1–3, explain in your own words why the writer believes that the English middle classes are being "hypocritical".

   2   U

   (*b*) Show how the writer's use of language in lines 4–10 creates a self-mocking tone.

   2   A

8. Show how the writer's use of language in lines 11–19 emphasises the extreme nature of the English middle classes' view of the threat to the countryside.

   In your answer you should refer to specific language features such as: imagery, word choice, register . . .

   4   A

9. Show how the writer's sentence structure **or** word choice in lines 20–24 emphasises his view that the threat to the countryside is much less serious than the English middle classes suggest.

   2   A

10. (*a*) According to lines 25–27, why does the writer believe "a quarter of the green belt around London" should be used for housing?

   2   U

   (*b*) How does the writer's use of language in lines 27 ("Because . . .") –32 cast doubt on the belief that green belts benefit everyone?

   2   A

11. In lines 33–43 the writer criticises two further arguments put forward by the "green-belt protectionists".

   Choose **either** the argument discussed in lines 33–37 **or** the argument discussed in lines 38–43, and answer **both** of the following questions on the paragraph you have chosen.

   (*a*) Explain why, in the writer's opinion, the green-belt protectionists' argument is flawed.

   2   U

   (*b*) How effective do you find the writer's use of language in conveying his attitude to their argument?

   2   A/E

12. How effective do you find lines 44–49 as a conclusion to the writer's attack on the attitudes of "middle-class homeowners"?

   2   E

   (20)

Question on both Passages

13. In Passage 1 David Sinclair refers to the claims of conservationists as "palpably nonsensical" and in Passage 2 Richard Morrison states that their views are "hogwash". Which writer is more successful in convincing you that these conservationists' claims are seriously flawed?

   Justify your choice by referring to the **ideas and/or style** of **both passages**.

   5   E

   (5)

   Total (50)

[END OF QUESTION PAPER]

[BLANK PAGE]

X115/303

NATIONAL
QUALIFICATIONS
2008

THURSDAY, 15 MAY
10.50 AM – 12.20 PM

ENGLISH
HIGHER
Critical Essay

Answer **two** questions.

Each question must be taken from a different section.

Each question is worth 25 marks.

Answer TWO questions from this paper. Each question must be chosen from a different Section (A–E). You are not allowed to choose two questions from the same Section.

In all Sections you may use Scottish texts.

Write the number of each question in the margin of your answer booklet and begin each essay on a fresh page.

You should spend about 45 minutes on each essay.

The following will be assessed:

- the relevance of your essays to the questions you have chosen, and the extent to which you sustain an appropriate line of thought

- your knowledge and understanding of key elements, central concerns and significant details of the chosen texts, supported by detailed and relevant evidence

- your understanding, as appropriate to the questions chosen, of how relevant aspects of structure/style/language contribute to the meaning/effect/impact of the chosen texts, supported by detailed and relevant evidence

- your evaluation, as appropriate to the questions chosen, of the effectiveness of the chosen texts, supported by detailed and relevant evidence

- the quality of your written expression and the technical accuracy of your writing.

SECTION A—DRAMA

Answers to questions on drama should address relevantly the central concern(s)/theme(s) of the text and be supported by reference to appropriate dramatic techniques such as: conflict, characterisation, key scene(s), dialogue, climax, exposition, dénouement, structure, plot, setting, aspects of staging (such as lighting, music, stage set, stage directions . . .), soliloquy, monologue . . .

1. Choose a play in which a central character is heroic yet vulnerable.

   Show how the dramatist makes you aware of both qualities and discuss how they affect your response to the character's fate in the play as a whole.

2. Choose a play which explores the theme of love in difficult circumstances.

   Explain how the dramatist introduces the theme and discuss how in the course of the play he/she prepares you for the resolution of the drama.

3. Choose from a play a scene in which an important truth is revealed.

   Briefly explain what the important truth is and assess the significance of its revelation to your understanding of theme or character.

4. Choose a play in which a character has to exist in a hostile environment.

   Briefly describe the environment and discuss the extent to which it influences your response to the character's behaviour and to the outcome of the play.

SECTION B—PROSE

Prose Fiction

> *Answers to questions on prose fiction should address relevantly the central concern(s)/theme(s) of the text(s) and be supported by reference to appropriate techniques of prose fiction such as: characterisation, setting, key incident(s), narrative technique, symbolism, structure, climax, plot, atmosphere, dialogue, imagery . . .*

5. Choose a **novel** which explores the cruelty of human nature.

   Show how the writer explores this theme and discuss how its exploration enhances your appreciation of the novel as a whole.

6. Choose a **novel** in which a confrontation between two characters is of central importance in the text.

   Explain the circumstances of the confrontation and discuss its importance to your understanding of the novel as a whole.

7. Choose **two short stories** which you appreciated because of the surprising nature of their endings.

   Compare the techniques used in creating these surprising endings and discuss which ending you feel is more successful as a conclusion.

8. Choose a **novel** or **short story** which is set during a period of social or political change.

   Discuss how important the writer's evocation of the period is to your appreciation of the text as a whole.

Prose Non-fiction

> *Answers to questions on prose non-fiction should address relevantly the central concern(s)/theme(s) of the text and be supported by reference to appropriate techniques of prose non-fiction such as: ideas, use of evidence, selection of detail, point of view, stance, setting, anecdote, narrative voice, style, language, structure, organisation of material . . .*

9. Choose a **non-fiction text** which you consider inspiring or provocative.

   Explain how the writer's presentation of his/her subject has such an impact on you.

10. Choose a piece of **travel writing** which offers surprising or amusing insights into a particular country or culture.

    Explain briefly what you learn about the country or culture and in greater detail discuss the techniques the writer uses to surprise or amuse you.

11. Choose a **non-fiction text** in which you consider the writer's stance on a particular issue to be ambiguous.

    Show how the writer's presentation of this issue illustrates the ambiguity of her/his stance.

[Turn over

SECTION C—POETRY

Answers to questions on poetry should address relevantly the central concern(s)/theme(s) of the text(s) and be supported by reference to appropriate poetic techniques such as: imagery, verse form, structure, mood, tone, sound, rhythm, rhyme, characterisation, contrast, setting, symbolism, word choice . . .

12. Choose a poem which deals with conflict or danger or death.

    Show how the poet creates an appropriate mood for the subject matter and go on to discuss how effectively she/he uses this mood to enhance your understanding of the central idea of the poem.

13. Choose a poem which is strongly linked to a specific location.

    Show how the poet captures the essence of the location and exploits this to explore an important theme.

14. Choose **two** poems which explore human relationships.

    By referring to both poems, discuss which you consider to be the more convincing portrayal of a relationship.

15. Choose a poem in which the speaker's personality is gradually revealed.

    Show how, through the content and language of the poem, aspects of the character gradually emerge.

SECTION D—FILM AND TV DRAMA

> *Answers to questions on film and TV drama should address relevantly the central concern(s)/theme(s) of the text(s) and be supported by reference to appropriate techniques of film and TV drama such as: key sequence(s), characterisation, conflict, structure, plot, dialogue, editing/montage, sound/soundtrack, aspects of mise-en-scène (such as lighting, colour, use of camera, costume, props . . .), mood, setting, casting, exploitation of genre . . .*

16. Choose a **film** or **TV drama*** in which a particular sequence is crucial to your understanding of an important theme.

    By referring to the sequence and to the text as a whole, show why you consider the sequence to be so important to your understanding of the theme.

17. Choose a **film** or **TV drama*** which presents a life-affirming story.

    By referring to key elements of the text, show how the story has such an effect.

18. Choose a **film** or **TV drama*** in which intense feelings have tragic consequences.

    Show to what extent the film or programme makers' presentation of these feelings and their consequences is successful in engaging you with the text.

19. Choose a **film** or **TV drama*** in which a complex character is revealed.

    Show how the film or programme makers reveal the complexity and discuss to what extent this aspect of the character contributes to your response to the text.

*"TV drama" includes a single play, a series or a serial.

[Turn over

SECTION E—LANGUAGE

Answers to questions on language should address relevantly the central concern(s) of the language research/study and be supported by reference to appropriate language concepts such as: register, jargon, tone, vocabulary, word choice, technical terminology, presentation, illustration, accent, grammar, idiom, slang, dialect, structure, point of view, orthography, abbreviation . . .

20. Consider uses of language designed to interest you in a social or commercial or political campaign.

Identify aspects of language which you feel are intended to influence you and evaluate their success in raising your awareness of the subject of the campaign.

21. Consider the spoken language of a clearly defined group of people.

Identify features which differentiate this language from standard usage and assess the extent to which these features have useful functions within the group.

22. Consider the language of newspaper reporting on such subjects as fashion, celebrities, reality TV, soap stars. . .

Identify some of the characteristics of this language and discuss to what extent it is effective in communicating with its target audience.

23. Consider the language (written and/or symbolic) associated with the use of e-mails or text messaging or instant messaging.

Describe some of the conventions associated with any one of these and discuss to what extent these conventions lead to more effective communication.

[END OF QUESTION PAPER]

[BLANK PAGE]

X115/301

NATIONAL
QUALIFICATIONS
2009

FRIDAY, 15 MAY
9.00 AM – 10.45 AM

ENGLISH
HIGHER
Close Reading—Text

There are TWO passages and questions.

Read the passages carefully and then answer all the questions, which are printed in a separate booklet.

You should read the passages to:

understand what the writers are saying about issues surrounding our use of natural resources (**Understanding—U**);

analyse their choices of language, imagery and structures to recognise how they convey their points of view and contribute to the impact of the passage (**Analysis—A**);

evaluate how effectively they have achieved their purpose (**Evaluation—E**).

PASSAGE 1

The first passage is from an article in The Telegraph *newspaper in January 2007. In it, Janet Daley responds to suggestions that we should limit our use of natural resources.*

A DOOMSDAY SCENARIO?

Is your journey really necessary? Who would have thought that, in the absence of world war and in the midst of unprecedented prosperity, politicians would be telling us not to travel? Just as working people have begun to enjoy the freedoms that the better-off have known for generations—the experience of other cultures, other
5 cuisines, other climates—they are threatened with having those liberating possibilities priced out of their reach.

And when I hear politicians—most of them comfortably off—trying to deny enlightenment and pleasure to "working class" people, I reach for my megaphone. Maybe Tommy Tattoo and his mates do use cheap flights to the sunshine as an
10 extension of their binge-drinking opportunities, but for thousands of people whose parents would never have ventured beyond Blackpool or Rothesay, air travel has been a social revelation.

So, before we all give the eco-lobby's anti-flying agenda the unconditional benefit of the doubt, can we just review their strategy as a whole?

15 Remember, it is not just air travel that the green tax lobby is trying to control: it is a restriction on any mobility. Clamping down on one form of movement, as the glib reformers have discovered, simply creates intolerable pressure on the others. Londoners, for example, had just become accustomed to the idea that they would have to pay an £8 congestion charge to drive into their own city when they
20 discovered that the fares on commuter rail and underground services had been hiked up with the intention of driving away customers from the public transport system—now grossly overcrowded as a result of people having been forced off the roads by the congestion charge.

The only solution—and I am just waiting for the politicians to recommend it
25 explicitly—is for none of us to go anywhere. Stay at home and save the planet. But that would be a craven retreat from all the social, professional and cultural interactions that unrestricted mobility makes possible—and which, since the Renaissance, have made great cities the centres of intellectual progress.

Even devising a way of making a living while never leaving your house would not
30 absolve you of your ecological guilt, because you'd still be making liberal use of the technology that has transformed domestic life. The working classes, having only discovered in the last generation or two the comforts of a tolerable degree of warmth and plentiful hot water, are now being told that these things must be rationed or prohibitively taxed.

35 Never mind that the universal presence of adequate heating has almost eliminated those perennial scourges of the poor—bronchitis and pneumonia—which once took the very young and the very old in huge numbers every winter. Never mind that the generous use of hot water and detergent, particularly when combined in a washing machine for the laundering of bed linen and clothing, has virtually eliminated the
40 infestations of body lice and fleas (which once carried plague) that used to be a commonplace feature of poverty. Never mind that the private car, the Green Public Enemy Number One, has given ordinary families freedom and flexibility that would have been inconceivable in previous generations.

If politicians are planning restrictions on these "polluting" aspects of private life, to
45 be enforced by a price mechanism, they had better accept that they will be
reconstructing a class divide that will drastically affect the quality of life of those on
the wrong side of it.

It is certainly possible that the premises advanced by environmental campaigners are
sound: that we are in mortal danger from global warming and that this is a result of
50 human activity. Yet when I listen to ecological warnings such as these, I am
reminded of a doomsday scenario from the past.

In his *Essay on the Principle of Population*, published in 1798, Thomas Malthus
demonstrated, in what appeared to be indisputable mathematical terms, that
population growth would exceed the limits of food supply by the middle of the 19th
55 century. Only plague, war or natural disaster would be capable of sufficiently
reducing the numbers of people to avert mass starvation within roughly 50 years.
This account of the world's inevitable fate (known as the "Malthusian catastrophe")
was as much part of accepted thinking among intellectuals then as are the
environmental lobby's warnings today.

60 Malthus, however, had made a critical conceptual mistake: he underestimated the
complexity of human behaviour. Population did not go on increasing at the same
rate; it responded to economic and social conditions. Moreover, he had discounted
the force of ingenuity in finding ways to increase food supply. In actual fact, the
introduction of intensive farming methods and the invention of pesticides
65 transformed what he had assumed would be the simple, fixed relation between
numbers of people and amount of resource. He had made what seemed to be a
sound prediction without allowing for the possibility that inventiveness and
innovation might alter the picture in unimaginable ways.

Warnings of catastrophe come and go. Whatever their validity, we cannot and
70 should not ask people to go back to a more restricted way of life. The restrictions
would not work anyway, because they are impracticable. If they were enforced, they
would be grotesquely unfair and socially divisive. If we really are facing an
environmental crisis, then we are going to have to innovate and engineer our way out
of it.

PASSAGE 2

Leo Hickman, writing in The Guardian *newspaper in May 2006, explores the ethics of leisure-
related flights.*

IS IT OK TO FLY?

I am desperate for some good news about aviation and its environmental impact.
Please someone say that they got the figures wrong. I have always loved the
freedom and access flying brings—who doesn't?—but in recent years I have
descended into near-permanent depression about how to square this urge with the
5 role of at least trying to be a responsible citizen of the planet. Travel is one of life's
pleasures, but is my future—and, more importantly, that of my two young
daughters—really going to be one of abstinence from flying, or at best flying by
quota, as many environmentalists are now calling for?

I recently travelled to Geneva to attend the second "Aviation and Environment
10   Summit" in search of, if not answers, then at least a better indication of just how
damaging flying really is to the environment. (The irony was not lost that hundreds
of people had flown from around the world to attend.)

Speaker after speaker bemoaned how the public had somehow misunderstood the
aviation industry and had come to believe that aviation is a huge and
15   disproportionate polluter. Let's get this in perspective, said repeated speakers: this
is small fry compared with cars, factories, even homes. Why are we being singled
out, they cried? Why not, they said, chase after other industries that could easily
make efficiency savings instead of picking on an industry that gives so much to the
world, yet is currently so economically fragile?

20   But even in this self-interested arena a representative from the US Federal Aviation
Administration caused some sharp intakes of breath from the audience by showing
an extraordinary map of current flightpaths etched over one another on the world's
surface. The only places on Earth that are not scarred by routes are blocks of air
space over the central Pacific, the southern Atlantic and Antarctica.

25   It seems, therefore, that we who avidly consume cheap flights do indeed have to face
a choice. Do we continue to take our minibreaks, visit our second homes, holiday on
the other side of the world and partake of all the other forms of what the industry
describes as "non-essential" travel? Or do we start to ration this habit, even if
others elsewhere in the world quite understandably will be quick to take our place
30   on the plane? My view is that flying will simply have to become more expensive.
Only by becoming more expensive will ticket prices start to reflect more closely the
environmental impact of flying—the polluter should always pay, after all—and
therefore drive down demand. It's easy to forget how good we've had it in this
heady era of low-cost carriers—but surely the good times must end.

35   A remedy such as carbon-neutralising our flights is a nice, cuddly idea that on the
surface is a positive action to take, but planting trees in Thailand or handing out
eco-lightbulbs in Honduras is no substitute for getting planes out of the skies. It
also carries the risk that people will think "job done" and simply carry on flying
regardless.

[END OF TEXT]

X115/302

| NATIONAL QUALIFICATIONS 2009 | FRIDAY, 15 MAY 9.00 AM – 10.45 AM | ENGLISH HIGHER Close Reading–Questions |

Answer all questions. **Use your own words whenever possible and particularly when you are instructed to do so.**

50 marks are allocated to this paper.

A code letter (U, A, E) is used alongside each question to give some indication of the skills being assessed. The number of marks attached to each question will give some indication of the length of answer required.

Questions on Passage 1

Marks   *Code*

1. (a) Referring to lines 1–6, give in your own words **two** reasons why the writer finds it surprising that politicians are "telling us not to travel". — 2   U

   (b) Show how the writer's sentence structure **and** word choice in lines 1–12 convey the strength of her commitment to air travel for all. — 4   A

2. Referring to specific words and/or phrases, show how the sentence "So, before . . . as a whole?" (lines 13–14) performs a linking function in the writer's argument. — 2   U

3. Read lines 15–23.

   (a) What, according to the writer, is the result of "Clamping down on one form of movement"? Use your own words in your answer. — 1   U

   (b) Explain how the writer uses the example of the London congestion charge to demonstrate her point. — 2   U

4. In the paragraph from lines 24 to 28, the writer states that "The only solution . . . is for none of us to go anywhere." (lines 24–25)

   (a) Why, according to the writer, is this "solution" undesirable? — 2   U

   (b) Show how, in this paragraph, the writer creates a tone which conveys her disapproval of the "solution". — 2   A

5. Read lines 29–47.

   (a) Why, according to the writer, would "never leaving your house" still involve some "ecological guilt"? — 1   U

   (b) Using your own words as far as possible, summarise the benefits of technology as described in lines 35–43. — 3   U

   (c) Show how the writer uses sentence structure in lines 35–43 to strengthen her argument. — 2   A

   (d) What, according to the writer in lines 44–47, would be the outcome of the restrictions proposed by politicians? — 2   U

6. Read lines 48–68.

   (a) What does the phrase "doomsday scenario" (line 51) mean? — 1   U

   (b) In your own words, outline the "doomsday scenario" predicted by Thomas Malthus. — 2   U

   (c) In your own words, give any **two** reasons why Malthus's theory proved incorrect. — 2   U

7. How effective do you find the writer's use of language in the final paragraph (lines 69–74) in emphasising her opposition to placing restrictions on people's way of life? — 2   A/E

(30)

		Marks	Code

Questions on Passage 2

8. (*a*) Explain the cause of the writer's "depression" (line 4). **2 U**

   (*b*) Show how the writer's use of language in lines 1–8 creates an emotional appeal to the reader. **2 A**

9. Read lines 9–24.

   (*a*) Explain the "irony" referred to in line 11. **1 U**

   (*b*) Show how the writer's use of language in lines 13–19 conveys his unsympathetic view of the speakers at the conference. In your answer you should refer to at least **two** features such as sentence structure, tone, word choice . . . **4 A**

   (*c*) How effective do you find the writer's use of imagery in lines 20–24 in conveying the impact that flying has on the environment? **2 A/E**

10. Explain why the writer believes that "flying will simply have to become more expensive" (line 30). **2 U**

11. Show how the writer, in lines 35–39, creates a dismissive tone when discussing possible remedies. **2 A**

   (15)

Question on both Passages

12. Which passage is more effective in engaging your interest in aspects of the environmental debate?

   Justify your choice by referring to the **ideas and style** of **both passages**. **5 E**

   (5)

   Total (50)

[END OF QUESTION PAPER]

[BLANK PAGE]

X115/303

NATIONAL
QUALIFICATIONS
2009

FRIDAY, 15 MAY
11.05 AM – 12.35 PM

ENGLISH
HIGHER
Critical Essay

Answer **two** questions.

Each question must be taken from a different section.

Each question is worth 25 marks.

Answer TWO questions from this paper. Each question must be chosen from a different Section (A–E). You are not allowed to choose two questions from the same Section.

In all Sections you may use Scottish texts.

Write the number of each question in the margin of your answer booklet and begin each essay on a fresh page.

You should spend about 45 minutes on each essay.

The following will be assessed:

- the relevance of your essays to the questions you have chosen, and the extent to which you sustain an appropriate line of thought

- your knowledge and understanding of key elements, central concerns and significant details of the chosen texts, supported by detailed and relevant evidence

- your understanding, as appropriate to the questions chosen, of how relevant aspects of structure/style/language contribute to the meaning/effect/impact of the chosen texts, supported by detailed and relevant evidence

- your evaluation, as appropriate to the questions chosen, of the effectiveness of the chosen texts, supported by detailed and relevant evidence

- the quality of your written expression and the technical accuracy of your writing.

SECTION A—DRAMA

Answers to questions on drama should address relevantly the central concern(s)/theme(s) of the text and be supported by reference to appropriate dramatic techniques such as: conflict, characterisation, key scene(s), dialogue, climax, exposition, dénouement, structure, plot, setting, aspects of staging (such as lighting, music, stage set, stage directions . . .), soliloquy, monologue . . .

1. Choose a play in which a central character behaves in an obsessive manner.

   Describe the nature of the character's obsessive behaviour and discuss the influence this behaviour has on your understanding of the character in the play as a whole.

2. Choose a play which you feel is made particularly effective by features of structure such as: dramatic opening, exposition, flashback, contrast, turning-point, climax, anticlimax, dénouement . . .

   Show how one or more than one structural feature employed by the dramatist adds to the impact of the play.

3. Choose from a play a scene which significantly changes your view of a character.

   Explain how the scene prompts this reappraisal and discuss how important it is to your understanding of the character in the play as a whole.

4. Choose a play set in a society whose values conflict with those of a central character or characters.

   Describe this difference in values and discuss how effectively the opposition of values enhances your appreciation of the play as a whole.

SECTION B—PROSE

Prose Fiction

> *Answers to questions on prose fiction should address relevantly the central concern(s)/theme(s) of the text(s) and be supported by reference to appropriate techniques of prose fiction such as: characterisation, setting, key incident(s), narrative technique, symbolism, structure, climax, plot, atmosphere, dialogue, imagery . . .*

5. Choose a **novel** or **short story** which deals with true love, unrequited love or love betrayed.

   Discuss the writer's exploration of the theme and show to what extent it conveys a powerful message about the nature of love.

6. Choose a **novel** or **short story** with a central character you consider to be heroic.

   Show how the heroic qualities are revealed and discuss how this portrayal of the character enhances your understanding of the text as a whole.

7. Choose a **novel** in which the setting in time and/or place is a significant feature.

   Show how the writer's use of setting contributes to your understanding of character and theme.

8. Choose a **novel** in which there is an incident involving envy or rivalry or distrust.

   Explain the nature of the incident and go on to discuss its importance to your understanding of the novel as a whole.

Prose Non-fiction

> *Answers to questions on prose non-fiction should address relevantly the central concern(s)/theme(s) of the text and be supported by reference to appropriate techniques of prose non-fiction such as: ideas, use of evidence, selection of detail, point of view, stance, setting, anecdote, narrative voice, style, language, structure, organisation of material . . .*

9. Choose an **essay** or a **piece of journalism** in which you feel that the writer's style is a key factor in developing a persuasive argument.

   Show how the writer's presentation of the argument is made persuasive by his or her use of techniques of non-fiction.

10. Choose a **full-length work** of **biography** or of **autobiography** in which the writer presents the life of her or his subject in a positive light.

    Show how the writer's style and skilful selection of material contribute to this positive portrayal.

11. Choose a **non-fiction text** which exploits the humour of particular situations and/or incidents.

    Show how the writer's use of humour creates interest in the subject matter.

SECTION C—POETRY

Answers to questions on poetry should address relevantly the central concern(s)/theme(s) of the text(s) and be supported by reference to appropriate poetic techniques such as: imagery, verse form, structure, mood, tone, sound, rhythm, rhyme, characterisation, contrast, setting, symbolism, word choice . . .

12. Choose a poem in which the poet explores one of the following emotions: anguish, dissatisfaction, regret, loss.

    Show how the poet explores the emotion and discuss to what extent he or she is successful in deepening your understanding of it.

13. Choose **two** poems which explore the experience of war.

    Discuss which you find more effective in conveying the experience of war.

14. Choose a poem in which contrast is important in developing theme.

    Explore the poet's use of contrast and show why it is important in developing a key theme of the poem.

15. Choose a poem which depicts a particular stage of life, such as childhood, adolescence, middle age, old age.

    Discuss how effectively the poet evokes the essence of this stage of life.

SECTION D—FILM AND TV DRAMA

> *Answers to questions on film and TV drama should address relevantly the central concern(s)/theme(s) of the text(s) and be supported by reference to appropriate techniques of film and TV drama such as: key sequence(s), characterisation, conflict, structure, plot, dialogue, editing/montage, sound/soundtrack, aspects of mise-en-scène (such as lighting, colour, use of camera, costume, props . . .), mood, setting, casting, exploitation of genre . . .*

16. Choose a **film** or **TV drama*** in which two characters are involved in a psychological conflict which dominates the text.

    Show how the film or programme makers reveal the nature of the conflict and explain why it is so significant to the text as a whole.

17. Choose from a **film** an important sequence in which excitement is created as much by filmic technique as by action and dialogue.

    Show how the film makers create this excitement and explain why the sequence is so important to the film as a whole.

18. Choose a **film** or **TV drama*** which evokes a particular period of history and explores significant concerns of life at that time.

    By referring to selected sequences and to the text as a whole, show how the film or programme makers evoke the period and explore significant concerns of life at that time.

19. Choose one or more than one **film** which in your opinion demonstrate(s) outstanding work by a particular director.

    By referring to key elements of the text(s), show why you consider the work of this director to be so impressive.

*"TV drama" includes a single play, a series or a serial.

[**Turn over**

SECTION E—LANGUAGE

Answers to questions on language should address relevantly the central concern(s) of the language research/study and be supported by reference to appropriate language concepts such as: register, jargon, tone, vocabulary, word choice, technical terminology, presentation, illustration, accent, grammar, idiom, slang, dialect, structure, point of view, orthography, abbreviation . . .

20. Consider aspects of language which change over time, such as slang, idiom, dialect . . .

Identify some of the changes and discuss to what extent you feel these changes contribute towards possible problems in communication between different age groups or generations.

21. Consider some of the changes in language which have occurred as a result of lobbying by pressure groups such as feminists, multi-cultural organisations, faith groups . . .

By examining specific examples, discuss to what extent you feel that clarity of communication has been affected by such changes.

22. Consider the use of persuasive language in the promotion of goods or services or a campaign or a cause.

By examining specific examples, evaluate the success of the language in achieving its purpose.

23. Consider the technical language associated with a sport, a craft, a profession or one of the arts.

By examining specific examples, discuss to what extent you feel such language leads to clearer communication.

[END OF QUESTION PAPER]

HIGHER

2010

[BLANK PAGE]

X115/301

| NATIONAL QUALIFICATIONS 2010 | WEDNESDAY, 12 MAY 9.00 AM – 10.45 AM | ENGLISH HIGHER Close Reading—Text |

There are TWO passages and questions.

Read the passages carefully and then answer all the questions, which are printed in a separate booklet.

You should read the passages to:

understand what the writers are saying about the changing nature of cities (**Understanding—U**);

analyse their choices of language, imagery and structures to recognise how they convey their points of view and contribute to the impact of the passage (**Analysis—A**);

evaluate how effectively they have achieved their purpose (**Evaluation—E**).

SQA

PASSAGE 1

In this passage, the journalist Deyan Sudjic, writing in The Observer *newspaper in March 2008, considers the irresistible growth of cities in the modern world.*

THE FUTURE OF THE CITY

In a world changing faster now than ever before, the dispossessed and the ambitious are flooding into cities swollen out of all recognition. Poor cities are struggling to cope. Rich cities are reconfiguring themselves at breakneck speed. China has created an industrial powerhouse from what were fishing villages in the 1970s. Lagos and Dhaka
5 attract a thousand new arrivals every day. In Britain, central London's population has started to grow again after 50 years of decline.

We have more big cities now than at any time in our history. In 1900, only sixteen had a population of one million; now it's more than 400. Not only are there more of them, they are larger than ever. In 1851, London had two million people. It was the largest
10 city in the world by a long way, twice the size of Paris, its nearest rival. That version of London would seem like a village now. By the official definition, London has getting on for eight million people, but in practical terms, it's a city of 18 million, straggling most of the way from Ipswich to Bournemouth in an unforgiving rash of business parks and designer outlets, gated housing and logistics depots.

15 Having invented the modern city, 19th century Britain promptly reeled back in horror at what it had done. To the Victorians exploring the cholera-ridden back alleys of London's East End, the city was a hideous tumour sucking the life out of the countryside and creating in its place a vast polluted landscape of squalor, disease and crime. In their eyes, the city was a place to be feared, controlled and, if possible,
20 eliminated.

Such attitudes continue to shape thinking about the city. Yet, like it or not, at some point in 2008, the city finally swallowed the world. The number of people living in cities overtook those left behind in the fields. It's a statistic that seems to suggest some sort of fundamental species change, like the moment when mankind stopped being
25 hunter gatherers and took up agriculture.

The future of the city has suddenly become the only subject in town. It ranges from tough topics such as managing water resources, economic policy, transport planning, racial tolerance and law enforcement to what is usually presented as the fluffier end of the scale, such as making public spaces people want to spend time in and deciding the
30 colour of the buses. But it is this diversity which powerfully affirms the city as mankind's greatest single invention.

For all their agonies, cities must be counted as a positive force. They are an engine of growth, a machine for putting the rural poor onto the first rung of urban prosperity and freedom. Look at London, a city that existed for several centuries before anything
35 approximating England had been thought of. It has a far stronger sense of itself and its identity than Britain as a whole or England. It has grown, layer on layer, for 2000 years, sustaining generation after generation of newcomers.

You see their traces in the Spitalfields district, where a French Huguenot chapel became, successively, a synagogue and a mosque, tracking the movement of waves of
40 migrants from poverty to suburban comfort. London's a place without an apparent structure that has proved extraordinarily successful at growing and changing. Its old residential core, sheltering in the approaches to its Tower of London fortress, has made the transition into the world's busiest banking centre. Its market halls and power stations have become art galleries and piazzas. Its simple terraced streets, built for the

45 clerks of the Great Western Railway in Southall, have become home to the largest Sikh community outside India.

And all of these worlds overlap in space and time. London is different for all its people. They make the most of the elements in it that have meaning for them and ignore the rest. A city is an à la carte menu. That is what makes it different from a village, which
50 has little room for tolerance and difference. And a great city is one in which as many people as possible can make the widest of choices from its menu.

The cities that work best are those that keep their options open, that allow the possibility of change. The ones that are stuck, overwhelmed by rigid, state-owned social housing, or by economic systems that offer the poor no way out of the slums, are
55 in trouble. A successful city is one that makes room for surprises. A city that has been trapped by too much gentrification or too many shopping malls will have trouble generating the spark that is essential to making a city that works.

Successful cities are the ones that allow people to be what they want; unsuccessful ones try to force them to be what others want them to be. A city of freeways like Houston or
60 Los Angeles forces people to be car drivers or else traps them in poverty. A successful city has a public transport system that is easy to use; an unsuccessful city tries to ban cars.

A successful city has room for more than the obvious ideas about city life, because, in the end, a city is about the unexpected, about a life shared with strangers and open to
65 new ideas. An unsuccessful city has closed its mind to the future.

PASSAGE 2

The following passage is adapted from The Dreaming City, *a report about Glasgow's future produced by a political "think tank" in 2007.*

Glasgow is a city which has experienced constant change and adaptation, from its period as a great industrial city and as the Second City of Empire, to its latter day reinvention as the City of Culture and the Second City of Shopping. This is a city with pull, buzz, excitement, and a sense of style and its own importance. It has a
5 potent international reach and influence. Glasgow's story continually weaves in and out of a global urban tapestry: following the trade threads of Empire, there are nearly two dozen towns and cities around the world named after Glasgow—from Jamaica to Montana to Nova Scotia. And there is even a Glasgow on the moon.

Glasgow's constant proclamation of its present success story is justified on the basis
10 that it benefits the city: confidence will breed confidence, tourists will visit, businesses will relocate and students will enrol. But, despite the gains this approach has brought for Glasgow and cities like it, there are signs that the wind is starting to come out of the sails. What felt radical when Dublin, Barcelona and Glasgow embarked on the city makeover path in the late 1980s and early 1990s, now feels derivative and is delivering
15 diminishing returns. When every city has commissioned a celebrity architect and pedestrianised a cultural quarter, distinctiveness is reduced to a formula.

Yet "official" Glasgow continues to celebrate its new-found status as a shopping mecca and top tourist destination, revelling in the city's new role as a place for conspicuous consumption, affluent lifestyles and global city breaks. There are several problems
20 with this. One is that this is a city with historic and deep inequalities, a city of sharp

divisions in income, employment, life chances and health. Another is that it can be seen as promoting a way of living that is unsustainable in terms of people's disposable income and growing levels of debt. And yet another problem is the clutter of cities on the world-class trail with the same familiar formula supporting
25 their campaign—shopping, tourism, mega-events, cultural events, iconic architecture and casinos—leaving little room for distinctiveness.

The politicians and the Establishment talk the language of "opportunity", "choice" and "diversity" for the people of the city, but do not really believe in or practise them. They impose a set menu, rather than the choice offered "à la carte",
30 confident that they know best. For all the rhetoric about new ways of working, partnership and collaboration, there can still be a very old-fashioned top-down approach in parts of institutional Glasgow that retains a faith that experts and professionals must hold all the answers. There is an implicit belief that people are poor because of low aspirations and Glaswegians are unhealthy because they won't
35 accept responsibility, make the right choices and eat healthily.

This dichotomy between the powerful and the powerless undermines the whole concept of the "resurgence" of cities such as Glasgow. At the moment, the city and its people only come together for mega-events such as the Commonwealth Games or City of Music bids. The question is whether this unity can be mobilised in a more
40 sustained way. There is an urgent need to find some new shared values and vision to help bridge the gap between the city and its people—to close the gap between the cities people want and the cities people get.

[END OF TEXT]

X115/302

NATIONAL
QUALIFICATIONS
2010

WEDNESDAY, 12 MAY
9.00 AM – 10.45 AM

ENGLISH
HIGHER
Close Reading–Questions

Answer all questions.

50 marks are allocated to this paper.

A code letter (U, A, E) is used alongside each question to give some indication of the skills being assessed. The number of marks attached to each question will give some indication of the length of answer required.

When answering questions coded "U—Understanding", use your own words as far as is reasonably possible and do not simply repeat the wording of the passage.

Marks *Code*

Questions on Passage 1

> *You are reminded of the instruction on the front cover:*
> *When answering questions coded "U—Understanding", use your own words as far as is reasonably possible and do not simply repeat the wording of the passage.*

1. Read lines 1–6.

   (a) Explain which groups of people are being attracted to cities.　2　U

   (b) Show how any **two** examples of word choice in this paragraph emphasise the impact of the growth of cities.　2　A

2. Referring to lines 7–14, explain **two** ways in which "That version of London would seem like a village now" (lines 10–11).　2　U

3. Show how the writer's use of language in lines 15–20 conveys the Victorians' disgust at the city they had created. You should refer in your answer to such features as imagery, word choice, sentence structure . . .　4　A

4. In lines 21–25, the writer tells us that for the first time in history more people are now living in cities than in the countryside. Show how the writer's use of language in this paragraph emphasises the momentous nature of this change.　2　A

5. Read lines 26–31.

   Explain in detail why the writer thinks the city is "mankind's greatest single invention" (line 31).　2　U

6. Read lines 32–37.

   Give any **two** reasons why cities "must be counted as a positive force".　2　U

7. Read lines 38–46.

   (a) Explain how any **one** of the examples in these lines illustrates the surprising nature of the way London has changed over time.　2　U

   (b) Show how the sentence structure of the paragraph as a whole emphasises the idea of change.　2　A

8. Show how the image of the "à la carte menu" illustrates the point the writer is making in lines 47–51.　2　A

9. Read lines 52–65.

   (a) According to the writer, what is the key difference between successful cities and unsuccessful cities?　1　U

   (b) Show how the writer's use of language in these lines emphasises this difference.　2　A

   (25)

Marks *Code*

Questions on Passage 2

> *You are reminded of the instruction on the front cover:*
> *When answering questions coded "U—Understanding", use your own words as far as is*
> *reasonably possible and do not simply repeat the wording of the passage.*

10. Read lines 1–8.

  (*a*) Explain why, according to the writer, Glasgow was in the past an important world city.   1   U

  (*b*) Explain why Glasgow could be considered important now.   1   U

  (*c*) Show how the writer's use of language in lines 3–8 ("This is a city . . . the moon.") emphasises Glasgow's importance.   2   A

11. Read lines 9–16.

  (*a*) What does the writer mean by the words "radical" (line 13) and "derivative" (line 14) in his discussion of city development?   2   U

  (*b*) Show how the writer's use of language in lines 9–16 suggests his doubts about the alleged "success story" of Glasgow.   4   A

12. Read lines 17–26.

  (*a*) "There are several problems with this." (lines 19–20). Explain briefly what these "problems" are.   3   U

  (*b*) Explain fully how the structure of lines 19–26 ("There are . . . room for distinctiveness.") helps to clarify the writer's argument.   2   A

13. Read lines 27–35.

  (*a*) What is the writer's main criticism of the way the "politicians and the Establishment" run Glasgow?   1   U

  (*b*) Show how the writer's use of language in this paragraph creates a tone of disapproval.   2   A

14. Read lines 36–42.

  Explain the approach the writer would prefer to see in the way Glasgow is run.   2   U

(20)

Question on both Passages

15. Which passage do you think offers the more thought-provoking ideas about the nature of cities?

  Justify your choice by close reference to the **ideas** of **both passages**.   5   U/E

(5)

Total (50)

[END OF QUESTION PAPER]

[BLANK PAGE]

X115/303

NATIONAL
QUALIFICATIONS
2010

WEDNESDAY, 12 MAY
11.05 AM – 12.35 PM

ENGLISH
HIGHER
Critical Essay

Answer **two** questions.

Each question must be taken from a different section.

Each question is worth 25 marks.

Answer TWO questions from this paper. Each question must be chosen from a different Section (A–E). You are not allowed to choose two questions from the same Section.

In all Sections you may use Scottish texts.

Write the number of each question in the margin of your answer booklet and begin each essay on a fresh page.

You should spend about 45 minutes on each essay.

The following will be assessed:

- the relevance of your essays to the questions you have chosen, and the extent to which you sustain an appropriate line of thought

- your knowledge and understanding of key elements, central concerns and significant details of the chosen texts, supported by detailed and relevant evidence

- your understanding, as appropriate to the questions chosen, of how relevant aspects of structure/style/language contribute to the meaning/effect/impact of the chosen texts, supported by detailed and relevant evidence

- your evaluation, as appropriate to the questions chosen, of the effectiveness of the chosen texts, supported by detailed and relevant evidence

- the quality of your written expression and the technical accuracy of your writing.

SECTION A—DRAMA

Answers to questions on drama should address relevantly the central concern(s)/theme(s) of the text and be supported by reference to appropriate dramatic techniques such as: conflict, characterisation, key scene(s), dialogue, climax, exposition, dénouement, structure, plot, setting, aspects of staging (such as lighting, music, stage set, stage directions . . .), soliloquy, monologue . . .

1. Choose a play in which a central concern is clarified by the contrast between two characters.

    Discuss how the dramatist's presentation of the contrast between the two characters adds to your understanding of this central concern.

2. Choose a play in which a central character experiences not only inner conflict but also conflict with one (or more than one) other character.

    Explain the nature of both conflicts and discuss which one you consider to be more important in terms of character development and/or dramatic impact.

3. Choose from a play a scene in which tension builds to a climax.

    Explain how the dramatist creates and develops this tension, and discuss the extent to which the scene has thematic as well as dramatic significance.

4. Choose a play which explores one of the following as a central concern: sacrifice, courage, integrity, steadfastness of purpose.

    Show how the dramatist introduces and develops the central concern in a way which you find effective.

SECTION B—PROSE

Prose Fiction

> *Answers to questions on prose fiction should address relevantly the central concern(s)/theme(s) of the text(s) and be supported by reference to appropriate techniques of prose fiction such as: characterisation, setting, key incident(s), narrative technique, symbolism, structure, climax, plot, atmosphere, dialogue, imagery . . .*

5. Choose a **novel** or **short story** which features a relationship between two characters which is confrontational or corrosive.

    Describe how the relationship is portrayed and discuss to what extent the nature of the relationship influences your understanding of the text as a whole.

6. Choose a **novel** in which the novelist makes use of more than one location.

    Discuss how the use of different locations allows the novelist to develop the central concern(s) of the text.

7. Choose a **novel** in which a character experiences a moment of revelation.

    Describe briefly what is revealed and discuss its significance to your understanding of character and/or theme.

8. Choose a **novel** in which a character seeks to escape from the constraints of his or her environment or situation.

    Explain why the character feels the need to escape and show how his or her response to the situation illuminates a central concern of the text.

9. Choose **two short stories** whose openings are crafted to seize the reader's attention.

    Explain in detail how the impact of the openings is created and go on to evaluate which of the stories develops more successfully from its opening.

Prose Non-fiction

> *Answers to questions on prose non-fiction should address relevantly the central concern(s)/theme(s) of the text and be supported by reference to appropriate techniques of prose non-fiction such as: ideas, use of evidence, selection of detail, point of view, stance, setting, anecdote, narrative voice, style, language, structure, organisation of material . . .*

10. Choose a work of **biography** or of **autobiography** which describes triumph over adversity or triumph over misfortune.

    Show how the writer's presentation of events and details in the subject's life leads you to an appreciation of her or his eventual success.

11. Choose a **non-fiction text** in which the writer's use of structure makes a significant impact.

    Describe the important structural features of the text and show how these enhance the impact of the writer's message.

12. Choose a **non-fiction text** in which vivid description is an important feature.

    Discuss in detail how the vivid description is created and go on to explain how it contributes to your appreciation of the text as a whole.

SECTION C—POETRY

Answers to questions on poetry should address relevantly the central concern(s)/theme(s) of the text(s) and be supported by reference to appropriate poetic techniques such as: imagery, verse form, structure, mood, tone, sound, rhythm, rhyme, characterisation, contrast, setting, symbolism, word choice . . .

13. Choose a poem in which the central concern(s) is/are clarified for you in the closing lines.

     Show how these closing lines provide an effective clarification of the central concern(s) of the poem.

14. Choose a poem in which there is an element of ambiguity.

     Show how the poet's use of ambiguity enriches your appreciation of the poem as a whole.

15. Choose a poem in which the creation of mood or atmosphere is an important feature.

     Show how the poet creates the mood or atmosphere, and discuss its importance in your appreciation of the poem as a whole.

16. Choose **two** poems in which differing stances are adopted on the same subject.

     Show how the stances are revealed and discuss which treatment you find more effective.

SECTION D—FILM AND TV DRAMA

Answers to questions on film and TV drama should address relevantly the central concern(s)/theme(s) of the text(s) and be supported by reference to appropriate techniques of film and TV drama such as: key sequence(s), characterisation, conflict, structure, plot, dialogue, editing/montage, sound/soundtrack, aspects of mise-en-scène (such as lighting, colour, use of camera, costume, props . . .), mood, setting, casting, exploitation of genre . . .

17. Choose a **film** or **TV drama*** in which a character overcomes apparently insuperable difficulties.

Briefly describe these difficulties and go on to discuss how the film or programme makers present the character's success in a way which you find satisfying.

18. Choose a **film** or **TV drama*** in which the opening sequence successfully establishes key features of the text such as setting, mood, genre, character . . .

By referring to more than one key feature in the sequence, show how the film or programme makers achieve this success and go on to discuss the importance of the sequence to your appreciation of the text as a whole.

19. Choose a **film** or **TV drama*** which portrays a family or group of people with a distinctive set of values.

Show how the film or programme makers reveal these values and discuss to what extent these contribute to your understanding of theme.

20. Choose a **film** or **TV drama*** which deals with violence but does not glorify it.

Discuss the film or programme makers' exploration of violence, making clear why you consider the treatment to be acceptable.

*"TV drama" includes a single play, a series or a serial.

[Turn over

SECTION E—LANGUAGE

Answers to questions on language should address relevantly the central concern(s) of the language research/study and be supported by reference to appropriate language concepts such as: register, jargon, tone, vocabulary, word choice, technical terminology, presentation, illustration, accent, grammar, idiom, slang, dialect, structure, point of view, orthography, abbreviation . . .

21. Consider aspects of language shared by members of a vocational group.

    Identify some examples of the language used within the group and evaluate the extent to which this shared language contributes to the effectiveness of the group's vocational activities.

22. Consider the language used to promote products, ideas or beliefs.

    Identify some of the characteristics of this language and assess how effective it is in promoting these products, ideas or beliefs.

23. Consider the language of broadsheet and/or tabloid newspaper reporting of a specific subject area such as politics, environmental issues, crime, sport, education . . .

    Identify some of the characteristics of this language and discuss its effectiveness in reporting on the chosen subject.

24. Consider the spoken language of a specific geographical area.

    Identify some of the characteristics of the language of your chosen area and discuss to what extent it enriches community life.

[END OF QUESTION PAPER]

[BLANK PAGE]

[BLANK PAGE]

[BLANK PAGE]

[BLANK PAGE]

[BLANK PAGE]

Acknowledgements

Permission has been sought from all relevant copyright holders and Bright Red Publishing is grateful for the use of the following:

The article 'The Shape of Things to Come' from www.economist.com, 11 December 2003 © The Economist Newspaper Limited, London 2003 (2006 Close Reading pages 2–3);

The article 'Foolish Panic is About Profit' by Susie Orbach, taken from The Observer, 30 May 2004. Reproduced by permission of Susie Orbach. (2006 Close Reading page 4);

An article adapted from 'Despite Google, we still need good libraries' by George Kerevan, taken from The Scotsman, 15 December 2004 © The Scotsman Publications Ltd. (2007 Close Reading pages 2–3);

The article 'Paradise is Paper, Vellum and Dust' by Ben Macintyre © The Times/NI Syndication, 18 December 2004 (2007 Close Reading pages 3–4);

Adapted extract taken from 'Shades of Green' by David Sinclair. Published by Grafton Books (Harper Collins). Reproduced with permission of David Sinclair (2008 Close Reading pages 2–3);

The article 'Yes, I will let Mr Prescott build in my backyard' by Richard Morrison © The Times/NI Syndication, 30 April 2004 (2008 Close Reading pages 3–4);

The article 'If Eco-Snobs had their way, none of us would go anywhere', by Janet Daley taken from The Telegraph © Telegraph Media Group Limited (8 January 2007) (2009 Close Reading pages 2–3);

The article 'Is it OK to fly?' by Leo Hickman, 20 May 2006. Copyright Guardian News & Media Ltd 2006 (2009 Close Reading pages 3–4).

The article 'Cities on the Edge of Chaos' by Deyan Sudjic, from The Observer, 9 March 2008. Copyright Guardian News & Media Ltd 2008 (2010 Close Reading pages 2–3);

An extract from 'The Dreaming City' by Gerry Hassan, Melissa Mean & Charlie Tims, 2007. Reproduced with permission of Demos (2010 Close Reading pages 3–4).